MOBY DICK

Herman Melville

Feb. 2005

AGS®

American Guidance Service, Inc.
Circle Pines, Minnesota 55014-1796
1-800-328-2560

AGS
Illustrated
CLASSICS

AGS ILLUSTRATED CLASSICS

Collection 1

Black Beauty, The Call of the Wild, Dr. Jekyll and Mr. Hyde, Dracula, Frankenstein, Huckleberry Finn, Moby Dick, The Red Badge of Courage, The Time Machine, Tom Sawyer, Treasure Island, 20,000 Leagues Under the Sea

Collection 2

The Great Adventures of Sherlock Holmes, Gulliver's Travels, The Hunchback of Notre Dame, The Invisible Man, Journey to the Center of the Earth, Kidnapped, The Mysterious Island, The Scarlet Letter, The Story of My Life, A Tale of Two Cities, The Three Musketeers, The War of the Worlds

Collection 3

Around the World in Eighty Days, Captains Courageous, A Connecticut Yankee in King Arthur's Court, The Hound of the Baskervilles, The House of the Seven Gables, Jany Eyre, The Last of the Mohicans, The Best of O. Henry, The Best of Poe, Two Years Before the Mast, White Fang, Wuthering Heights

Collection 4

Ben Hur, A Christmas Carol, The Food of the Gods, Ivanhoe, The Man in the Iron Mask, The Prince and the Pauper, The Prisoner of Zenda, The Return of the Native, Robinson Crusoe, The Scarlet Pimpernel, The Sea Wolf, The Swiss Family Robinson

Collection 5

Billy Budd, Crime and Punishment, Don Quixote, Great Expectations, Heidi, The Iliad, Lord Jim, The Mutiny on Board H.M.S. Bounty, The Odyssey, Oliver Twist, Pride and Prejudice, The Turn of the Screw

Shakespeare Collection

As You Like It, Hamlet, Julius Caesar, King Lear, Macbeth, The Merchant of Venice, A Midsummer Night's Dream, Othello, Romeo and Juliet, The Taming of the Shrew, The Tempest, Twelfth Night

Printed in the United States of America
ISBN 0-7854-0668-9 (Previously ISBN 1-56103-432-0)
Product Number 40349
A 0 9 8 7 6

to the reader

Welcome to the AGS Illustrated Classics!

You are about to enter the world of great literature through pictures as well as words. Now you can actually see the great characters of literature as you read about them!

We want you to know that the costumes, hairstyles, room furnishings, and landscapes have all been carefully researched. No detail has been left out.

As you read, notice that important words are marked with an asterisk (*) and defined at the bottom of the page. Also watch for the scrolls that appear now and then. The scrolls contain important information that will add to your enjoyment of the story.

Now sit back and relax. We know that you will enjoy a great reading experience in the pages that follow.

—The Editors

ABOUT THE AUTHOR

Herman Melville was born in 1819. His formal education ended in 1834, at age fifteen. For a time he was both clerk and school teacher, but the sea was his first love. He became a cabin boy on a merchant ship bound for England. Later, in 1841, Melville joined the crew of a whaling ship, the *Acushnet,* where he learned much of the background for *Moby Dick.*

Melville was influenced by the writing of Nathaniel Hawthorne and dedicated *Moby Dick* to him. Melville felt that Hawthorne had an insight into human nature that few could surpass.

Melville, too, knew mankind mainly from living in many cultures. His life with the Taipis, cannibal natives, led him to write *Typee.* From a mutiny he experienced, he wrote *Omoo.* One of his later books, and most heart rending is *Billy Budd*—the story of a young and severely abused seaman.

In spite of his unusual creative ability, Melville spent nineteen years of his life as a customs officer in the ports of New York City. Not until after his death was he truly appreciated as an author. Today *Moby Dick* is considered to be one of the greatest, if not the greatest, American novel.

Herman Melville

MOBY DICK

Adapted by
IRWIN SHAPIRO

Illustrated by
ALEX NINO

a
VINCENT FAGO
production

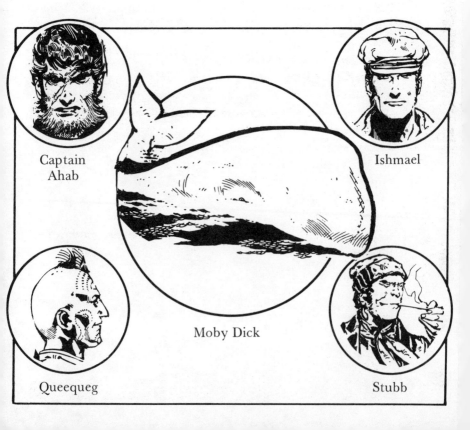

Captain
Ahab

Ishmael

Queequeg

Moby Dick

Stubb

Call me Ishmael.

Some years ago, with nothing to interest me on shore, I thought I would sail about a little and see the oceans of the world. I loved to sail dangerous seas and land on foreign coasts. I had already made a number of voyages on trading ships and now set out to go whaling. I had no idea I would meet the mad Captain Ahab and hunt for the great white whale which men called Moby Dick.

I landed in New Bedford on a Saturday night in December. I was very unhappy to learn that the boat for Nantucket had already sailed. There was no way of reaching Nantucket until Monday.

What a bitter night! I must find somewhere to stay.

I soon came to an inn.

Spouter? Coffin! Rather evil sounding—but I'll risk it.

Inside, I found the landlord.

My house is full. But wait! You have no objection to sharing a bed with a harpooneer, have you?

I'll share with any good man, rather than walk about on so bitter a night.

All right. Take a seat. You want supper?

Where is that harpooneer? Is he here?

He'll be here before long.

But at twelve o'clock the harpooneer still hadn't come in.

Landlord! Does he always keep such late hours?

No, but tonight he went out selling, and maybe he can't sell his head.

His head?

It's just a shrunken head. . .a strange thing, you know. . . but it's getting very late. You'd better be turning in.

I took the landlord's advice. But I had not been asleep long before I awakened and. . . .

Lord save me! The harpooneer!

First he prayed to a stone god. Then, undressing, he lit up a tomahawk which he used as a pipe.

Putting out the lamp, he jumped into bed.

Who-ee devil you? Speak or I kill!

Landlord, save me!

Why didn't you tell me he was a wild man?

Don't be afraid. Queequeg wouldn't harm a hair of your head.

After some thought.

Why be upset? He's a human being, just as I am. . .and a whaling man. Better to sleep with a sober wild man than a drunken Christian.

If you'll just put that tomahawk away, or pipe, or whatever it is.

Me do. . . you get in.

I never slept better in my life. Next morning, we had breakfast.

No coffee and rolls for him. . .only beefsteaks, rare.

12

Then we went to the Whaleman's Chapel, where we heard a special talk by Father Mapple.

Shipmates, sin not! But if you do, ask to be forgiven like Jonah!

Returning to the inn, we had a friendly smoke together.

We friends. We go whaling together.

And so, on Monday, we took the boat to Nantucket.

In Nantucket, Queequeg asked his stone god, Yojo, for help.

Yojo say you find-ee ship for us.

And so I set out among the many ships. Of the ships in port, I picked the Pequod. On deck, in a tent supported by whale bone, I found Captain Peleg, a Quaker and owner of one of the boats.

Sir, I was think ing of going out on a ship.

You were? What takes you a-whaling?

I want to see the world, and what whaling is.

What whaling is, eh? Have you seen Captain Ahab, who is captain of this ship? He has only one leg!

Was the other lost by a whale?

Chewed up, by the biggest whale that ever rammed a boat.

Do you still wish to go a-whaling? Then come below with me to Bildad, another owner, and sign the papers.

Reading the Bible again, Bildad, eh? He says he's our man and wants to sail.

Do you?

I do.

He'll do. But don't be too generous with the pay. Our duty is to the other owners of this ship, many of them widows and orphans.

Blast ye, Bildad, I'll not cheat this young man!

I have a friend who wants to sail, too. He has killed more whales than I can count.

Bring him along, then.

And so, the next day. . . .

What a harpoon he's got! I say Quohog, or whatever your name is, did you ever spear a fish?

Queequeg jumped into a whale-boat hanging at the side.

You see small drop of tar on water. Suppose it whale eye. Watch then!

If him whale eye—why, the whale dead!

Quick, Bildad, get the ship's papers! We must have Hedgehog there, I mean Quohog! And we'll give him more than ever was given a harpooneer out of Nantucket!

As we left the ship we met an old sailor.

Have you signed up with that ship? And have you seen Captain Ahab?

We haven't. They say he's sick, but will soon be all right.

Ha! When Captain Ahab is all right, then this left arm of mine will be all right, not before!

Come Queequeg. . . this fellow is crazy.

Morning to you, shipmates . . .and God pity you! God pity you!

For several days we were very busy on the Pequod. Supplies for a three years' voyage were brought on board the ship.

Then, on a cold Christmas day, we sailed, with Bildad and Peleg to lead us out of the port.

Man the anchor! Blood and thunder... jump!

Move it, you men! Pull and lift it, you men. Heave, thou Quohog!

At last Peleg and Bildad said their good-byes and got into the pilot boat. Ship and boat moved in different directions, and we sailed into the wide Atlantic, not knowing what waited for us out there.

We were a crew from many countries.

Our officers were Chief Mate Starbuck — tall, and careful. . . .

Happy-go-lucky Stubb, the Second Mate. . . .

And Flask, the Third Mate, who lived to kill.

But for several days nothing was seen of Captain Ahab.

Then one day, I saw him on the quarter-deck. Something about him made me afraid.

Not long after, Ahab gave an order usually only for emergencies. . . .

The entire ship's company came together.

Send everybody to the rear!

Sir? Yes, sir, everybody to the rear.

You have heard me give orders about a white whale. Look you! Do you see this coin of gold?

He nailed the coin to the main mast.

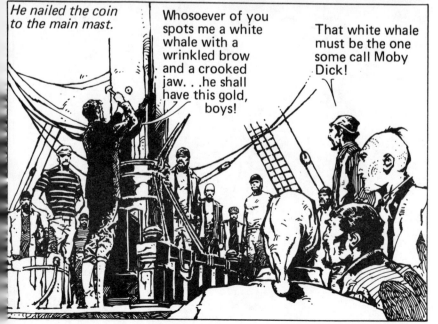

Whosoever of you spots me a white whale with a wrinkled brow and a crooked jaw. . .he shall have this gold, boys!

That white whale must be the one some call Moby Dick!

Was it not Moby Dick that took off your leg?

Who told you that?

Aye, it was that Moby Dick! Aye, aye! I'll chase him around the world before I give up! And this is what you have sailed for, men! To chase the white whale till he spits black blood. What say you men?

Aye! Aye!

We'll keep a sharp eye for the white whale!

A sharp harpoon for Moby Dick!

God bless you, men! Steward, go bring a small barrel of rum for the men.

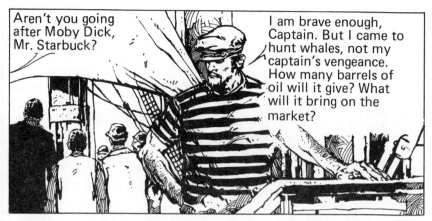

Aren't you going after Moby Dick, Mr. Starbuck?

I am brave enough, Captain. But I came to hunt whales, not my captain's vengeance. How many barrels of oil will it give? What will it bring on the market?

A curse on a dumb bully of an animal struck without knowing what he did! Madness! It goes against God.

Don't talk to me of God, man! I'd strike the sun if it insulted me! Some strange unknown power struck at me through the whale. . .shall I not strike back?

Ah, the barrel of rum! Drink men, and pass it on!

Drink well, me men! Drink and promise death to Moby Dick!

Death to Moby Dick!

God keep me! God keep us all!

Although Ahab's search was for Moby Dick, he did not forget the business of whaling. As we sailed south. . . .

Mastheads, keep a bright lookout! Sing out if you see a whale!

And one cloudy afternoon. . . .

There she blows! There she blows! She blows!

The order to lower the boats into the water was given and we set out to find the whale.

I was in Starbuck's boat and soon. . . .

Row, boys, row! There's a storm coming, but we've still time to kill a whale!

That's his hump. There, there, give it to him, Queequeg!

The storm struck. The whale rolled like an earthquake under us and escaped.

All night we floated in our water-filled boat. . . .

At dawn. . . .

Look out men! Jump!

Our own ship had hit us in the dark but we were quickly rescued.

But there were other days, and other whales. On one chase, Stubb's boat led the rest.

Give it to him, Tashtego!

Changing places with the harpooneer, Stubb dug his spear into the whale.

The whale went into its flurry, churning the water. . . .

Until. . . .

He's dead, Mr. Stubb.

Yes, he's stopped blowing water.

The whale was pulled to the ship.

Then the men tied it to the side of the Pequod with chains.

The head was cut off and dropped over the back of the ship, where it was held by a chain.

Next day, with hook and chain, the blubber was cut from the whale.

The peeled white body was cut loose and drifted away.

What a sad funeral for such a mighty animal!

The blubber was cut into smaller pieces!

Then the blubber was boiled down into oil in a large pot.

At night, in the darkness, the ship seemed to be on fire.

In the morning the whale's head was pulled up so that the very valuable oil called spermaceti could be taken from a case inside the head.

Tashtego climbed on top of the head and dug a hole with a sharp spade.

He pushed a bucket into the hole with a long pole.

Time and again the bucket was lifted up to the deck, where the oil was emptied into a tub.

Then. . .a slip of the foot. . . and. . . .

H-help!

Man overboard!

He fell into the case!

The head tore from the hooks, dropped, and slowly began to sink into the sea.

But Queequeg went to the rescue.

Soon he was under the water.

In a few moments. . . .

Look, he's got him!

Many a whale did we catch as we sailed southward, but Ahab had only one thought.

He heard a footstep at the door, and. . . .

We near Japan. . .these are the waters where Moby Dick may hide.

Who's there?

It is I, Starbuck, Captain Ahab.

Sir, oil is leaking from some barrels in the hold. We must stop and. . . .

What? Stop here for a week to repair old barrels.

If we do not, we will waste more oil in a day than we may get in a year. What will the owners say?

Owners? What do I care about the owners. Go on deck!

A better man than I might well pass over in you what he would resent in a young man. Aye, and in a happier man, too.

Do you dare to think wrongly of me? Get on deck!

Grabbing a loaded gun, Ahab aimed at Starbuck.

There is one God that is Lord over the earth, and one captain that is Lord over the Pequod. Now I order you to get on deck.

You have made me angry, sir, but you don't have to fear Starbuck. But Ahab should fear Ahab. Beware of yourself, old man.

What's that he said? Ahab, beware of Ahab. . .there's something true about what he says.

A little later on the deck. . . .

You are too good a fellow, Starbuck. Head for land and repair the barrel.

After the barrels were repaired the Pequod sailed on, and. . . .

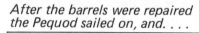

Blacksmith, make me a spear. . . one that will stick in a whale like his own fin-bone.

Is this harpoon for the white whale, sir?

Aye, for the white devil! Here. . . make the heads for the harpoon from my razors. I have no need of them, for I neither shave, eat, nor pray till. . .but here. . .to work!

Ahab made the harpoon ready, not in water, but in blood drawn from the harpooneers.

I baptize thee not in the name of the Father, but in the name of the devil!

As we sailed in the Japan seas, a storm broke on us from a cloudless sky.

By night, the ship's sails were torn. The sky and sea rocked with thunder and lightning.

As the men worked to save the ship. . . .

Who's there?

Old thunder! Ahab, the captain!

Look in the sky! Look at the sparks!

The metal and three pointed lightning rods on the masts glowed with a silent flame. Seamen called this the St. Elmo's fire.

Although the men had all seen this kind of thing before, they watched, frozen in their shoes.

God have mercy on us all!

It almost lights the way to the white whale!

Ahab held the chain of the main-mast lightning rod.

I will pretend to feel the pulse, and let mine beat against it. . .blood against fire! Leap up, fire! I leap with thee, worship thee!

Thy harpoon, captain! It glows with a ball of fire!

God is against thee, old man! This voyage will end in no good. Turn back!

Aye, let us sail home while we may!

But Ahab held the burning harpoon!

All of you promised to hunt for the white whale with me. We will all hunt, do you hear! Look here. . . .

With one breath he blew out the flame.

Thus I blow out the last fear!

The storm ended, and some hours later Starbuck went to Ahab's cabin to report that new sails had been put up and the ship was again on course.

He sleeps within. Shall I wake him . . .to drag us all to our doom?

He would have shot me. . .with this very gun!

Shall I let this crazy old man bring us all to our death? Would I be a murderer if. . . if. . . .

Then within the stateroom, Ahab cried out in his sleep.

Stern all! Oh, Moby Dick, I hold your heart at last!

No. . .no, I cannot. . . even though any day I may sink with all the crew to the bottom of the sea.

Sailing on, the Pequod met the Rachel, another whaler from Nantucket.

Have you seen the white whale?

Aye, yesterday.

RACHEL

The captain of the Rachel came aboard the Pequod.

The captain went back to the Rachel, to continue the search. We watched her as we sailed swiftly away. . . .

They haven't found the lost boy. . .I doubt they ever will.

A few days later. . . .

Moby Dick is around here. I must have the first sight of him myself! Make me a seat and raise me to the masthead!

From his high seat on top of the mast Ahab watched the sea.

Show yourself, you monster! Ahab challenges Moby Dick!

Not long after. . . .

A mild day, Starbuck. On such a sweet day I struck my first whale . . .forty years ago. Out of those forty years I have not spent three ashore. I have grown old and tired on the uncaring sea!

So little time have I spent on land. . .my wife's been alone since I wed her. What a forty years' fool has old Ahab been!

In your eyes, as in a magic glass, I see my home. . .and yours! Stay aboard the Pequod when Ahab gives chase to Moby Dick! The danger shall not be yours. You shall live to see home again!

Oh, my captain! Give up the chase of that hated monster! Let us turn back, and you, too, shall see home again!

Some nameless thing keeps me here. Some hidden lord and master drives me on . . .I dare not turn back.

Silently, without hope, Starbuck slipped away.

That night, Ahab suddenly smelled the sea air. . . .

That strange odor. . .it's a whale! Moby Dick is near!

Next morning, he ordered all hands on deck.

See you nothing? No sign of the white whale? Pull me aloft!

As he was pulled up the main mast. . . .

There she blows! A hump like a snow-hill! It is Moby Dick! I saw him first! The gold coin is mine! Lower me. . .quick!

Soon. . . .

Lower the boats! Boats, boats! Mr. Starbuck, remember, stay on board the ship!

As the boats raced toward the monster. . . .

There! He sounds!

Changing places, Ahab went to the bow and looked down.

I see his open jaw just below! Stand close to the stern!

The whale swam upwards, turning on its back, and. . . .

Look out, captain!

His jaws slowly closed on the boat. . .but one of his teeth caught on an oarlock.

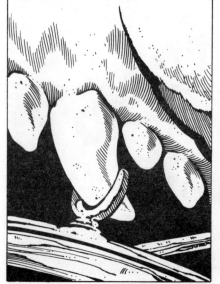

Ahab grabbed the long tooth trying to work it free.

Blast it, to hold me helpless in your very jaws.

Suddenly the jaws slipped from him, and. . . .

The whale caused the water to turn so that Ahab barely kept above it.

Then the Pequod, which had been standing by, sailed up.

Sail on the whale! Drive him away!

The whale was driven off, and the boats flew to the rescue.

Next day, Ahab again sighted the whale.

There she blows! There she blows in the waves!

Look for the last time at the sun, Moby Dick! Thy hour and thy harpoon are at hand!

In a few moments. . . .

Lower the boats! Mr. Starbuck, stay aboard and look after the ship!

This time the whale rushed at the boats. . . .

. . . .then dashed his head against the bottom of Ahab's boat.

Again the Pequod rescued the men and boats.

Let me lean on you, Starbuck. . .my ivory leg is broken. But I will kill the white whale yet, even if I circle the world ten times; and even dive right through it!

Never will you capture him, old man! One of our men is lost. . .I saw him pulled down. Shall we all be pulled to the bottom of the sea? Give up this madness!

Though I like you for some strange reason, you are a fool. I must go on, lieutenant! I act under orders, I must obey and chase Moby Dick! I must!

The next day the weather was clear. After an hour's watching. . . .

There! She blows! I meet thee, this third time, Moby Dick!

Again Ahab gave the order for the chase, and. . . .

Starbuck! For the third time my ship starts upon this voyage!

Aye, sir, you will have it so.

As the boats started forward, Moby Dick turned the water furiously.

Rushing head on, the whale over-turned two boats, but left Ahab's almost without a scar.

While the two boats were brought aboard the ship to be repaired, Ahab's boat, alone, chased the whale.

The sharks are chewing up the oars!

They will last long enough! Pull on!

With a curse, Ahab threw the harpoon.

It sank deep, but the whale pushed on, and the line snapped.

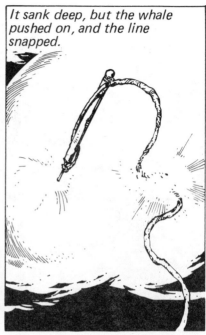

Suddenly, as the Pequod sailed up, the whale turned toward the ship.

The men on the Pequod saw the monster coming at them.

58

Death to my ship! Must she die? And without me? Am I not able to go down with my ship as is the wish of all brave captains? Oh lonely death after a lonely life.

Ho! Towards you I come, you monster whale. To the end of my life I will fight with you.

From my heart I stab you; for hate's sake I spit my last breath at you! Thus, I give up the spear!

Again the harpoon struck. The whale flew forward.

The line got tangled. Ahab bent to clear it, but the flying turn caught him around the neck.

He was shot out of the boat, and disappeared into the waves.

For an instant the boat's crew stood, as though in a trance.

Great God, where is the ship?

The ship, too, was disappearing into the ocean. And now drawn by the suction of the sinking ship, the small boat and all in it, and the smallest chip of the Pequod, were carried out of sight under the waves.

Then all was finished, and the great blanket of sea rolled on as it rolled five thousand years ago.

The story is done. But one did live through the wreck. . . I, Ishmael.

On the second day, a sail drew near. It was the Rachel, that in her search after her missing children, only found another orphan.

And I alone escaped to tell thee.

END

WORDS TO KNOW

blubber	harpooneer	vengeance
bow	stern	

QUESTIONS

1. Who tells the story of Moby Dick?

2. Why was Queequeg immediately hired as a harpooner on Ahab's ship?

3. Why did Ahab feel he had to catch the white whale?

4. Who tries to stop Ahab from chasing the white whale?

5. What was the prize Ahab offered to the first man to spot the white whale? Who spotted the whale first?

6. What became of Ahab's ship, the *Pequod?*

7. What is the name of the weapon actually used to kill a whale?

8. Why were whales hunted 100 years ago?

9. What is spermaceti?

10. Explain why you think Ahab was a good or a bad captain.